A PRACTICAL HANDBOOK OF PHARMACEUTICAL ENGINEERING

AS PER SYLLABUS PRESCRIBED FOR B. PHARMACY, SEMESTER-III BY PHARMACY COUNCIL OF INDIA, NEW DELHI

DR. SUNITA S. DEORE

Made with ♥ on the Notion Press Platform
www.notionpress.com

Contents

CHAPTER ONE

Experiment No. -1

Aim- Determination of radiation constant of brass, iron, unpainted and painted glass.

Requirements- Iron and Brass, metal cylinder, thermometer, wooden box, pair of tongs, tripod stand.

Principle- Heat is lost from hot cylinder surface to surrounding atmosphere by means of conduction and radiation. Heat transfer by radiation occurs, energy transfer through space by means of electromagnetic radiation (waves).Thus a body acts as an emitter, than energy being transmitted through the intervening spaces, and it is effective even in a perfect vacuum or inter-spacious space. The amount of thermal energy radiated by a surface is increased rapidly with increasing temperature, when a heat flows by actual mixing of warmer portions with cooler portions of the same material .This mechanism is known as Convection

Procedure-

1. Clean the iron cylinder, take weight of it. And note down.
2. Measure the diameter, height, radius and area of iron cylinder and temperature of room and record it.
3. Raise the temperature of iron cylinder by using burner upto 300°C.
4. After maximum temperature of 300°C is attained by the iron cylinder and temperature of room, record it
5. Keep the cylinder suddenly on wood block, place the thermometer at centre of the cylinder.
6. Record the change in temperature after each 10 minutes interval which decreases slowly till initial temperature of cylinder is attained.
7. Plot the graph of time on x-axis vs temperature in (°C) on y axis.
8. Slope of line dq/dt is calculated at various temperature which shows the rate of loss of heat from the hot cylinder.
9. Finally calculate the radiation constant.

Formula- qr

$$\sigma = \frac{qr}{Ar\,(T_1 - T_2)}$$

σ = Radiation constant

r = Emissivity constant

T_1 = Temperature of Metal body

T_2 = Temperature of Room

A. Area of radiating surface, m^2

q- energy radiated per second

Observations-

1. Mass of Iron cylinder, M_1=
2. Mass of Brass cylinder M_2
3. Rate of heat loss by iron cylinder dq/dt
4. Rate of heat loss by brass cylinder dq/dt
5. Temperature of metal body T_1

6. Temperature of the Room
7. Height of the Iron cylinder
8. Height of the Brass cylinder
9. Diameter of Iron cylinder
10. Diameter of Brass cylinder
11. Radius of the Iron cylinder
12. Radius of the Brass cylinder

Questions for viva-

1. Define conduction and convection.
2. Define convection and radiation.
3. State Fourier's law with equation of heat transfer.
4. What are objectives of heat transfer.
5. Give mechanisms of heat transfer

CHAPTER TWO

Experiment No.-2

Aim- To determine radiation constant of glass (unpainted and painted)

Requirements-

Round bottom flask (painted and unpainted), digital thermometer, beaker, tripod stand, wire gauze, etc.

Principle: Heat is lost from hot cylinder surface to surrounding atmosphere by means of conduction and radiation. Heat transfer by radiation occurs, energy transfer through space by means of electromagnetic radiation (waves).Thus a body acts as an emitter, than energy being transmitted through the intervening spaces, and it is effective even in a perfect vacuum or inter-spacious space. The amount of thermal energy radiated by a surface is increased rapidly with increasing temperature, when a heat flows by actual mixing of warmer portions with cooler portions of the same material .This mechanism is known as **Convection**

Procedure-

1. Select two round bottom flasks, one is painted, clean both the flasks properly.
2. Take weight of both flasks separately and note it down.
3. Measure diameter, average radius and surface area ($4\ \pi r^2$) of both the flasks and record it.
4. Tied the flasks separately to two stands.
5. Boil water and fill this hot water into each flasks upto the next mark.
6. Dip the thermometer to the centre of the flask to record the decrease in temperature after 10 min interval till room temperature is attained.
7. Graph is plotted as time on X-Axis vs temperature in degree Celsius on Y-axis.
8. Slope of the tangent is calculated, which gives the data about decrease in temperature.
9. This shows the rate of loss of heat from painted /unpainted round bottom flasks.
10. Calculate the radiation constant.

Formula –

$$\sigma = \frac{qr}{Ar\,(T_1^4 - T_2^4)}$$

σ = Radiation constant

r = Emissivity constant

T_1 = Temperature of Metal body

T_2 = Temperature of Room

A = Area of radiating surface, m^2

q- Energy radiated per second

Observations-

Mass of painted flask, M_1=

Mass of unpainted flask M_2

Rate of heat transforming dq/dt

Diameter of flask D

Radius of flask, r

Area of flask 4 πr^2

Temperature of the boiled water T_1

Temperature of the Room T_2

Questions for viva-

1. Give transfer of heat by radiation.
2. Define Radiation.
3. Define conduction.
4. What are the heat interchangers and heat exchangers?
5. What is Stefan-Boltzmann law?

CHAPTER THREE

Experiment No. -3

Aim- To calculate the efficiency of steam distillation.

Requirements- Steam generator, distillation flask, condenser, separating funnels, Nitrobenzene, double holed rubber cork, measuring cylinder, thermometer, Bent tubes, weighing balance and weights.

Chemical- Sodium chloride.

Principle- Steam distillation is method of distillation carried out with steam. It is used to separate high boiling substances from non-volatile impurities and immiscible liquids. When two immiscible liquids are boiled together neither substance appreciably influences the vapour pressure of the other. Each liquid exerts the same vapour pressure it would if heated alone.

Procedure-

1. Measure and take 50 ml of nitrobenzene in a distillation flask.
2. Close the flask with two holed rubber cork. Insert thermometer through one of the holes and fix.
3. Through the other hole, fix a bent tube of the steam generator for the steam to pass into the distillation flask.
4. Ensure the bent tube reaches almost near bottom of the flask but not touching the flask.
5. Fix the side tube of the neck of distillation flask to condenser.
6. Now allow the steam to pass into the distillation flask continuously from the steam generator.
7. When the thermometer shows constant temperature at which the mixture of nitrobenzene and steam distils, collect distillate for 10 min. into previously weighed beaker.
8. Determine the weight of the mixture and beaker.
9. Transfer the distillate into separate funnel and add few grams of sodium chloride. Shake the funnel vigorously till nitrobenzene and water get separated.
10. Collect nitrobenzene separately and denote its weight.
11. Collect water separately and denote its weight.

Questions for viva-

1 What is the purpose of steam distillation?

1. Give principle behind steam distillation.
2. Define steam distillation.
3. Give applications of steam distillation.

CHAPTER FOUR

Experiment No.-4

Aim- To construct drying curve for calcium carbonate.

Requirements- Spatula, glass rod, pen, pencil, record book, calculator, Graph paper, Hot air oven, petridish, thermometer, weighing balance.

Chemicals- Calcium carbonate

Principle- To behaviour of drying of solid is explained by drying curve. The time required for drying a batch of weight of martial in a dry air can be estimated with the help of drying curve. Drying is a mass transfer process consists of the removal of water or other solvent by evaporations from a solid, semisolid or liquid. This process is obtained used as final production steps before, packing products.

Procedure-

1. Take and weigh empty, clean petri plate and record it as W_1.
2. Calculate the area of petri plate by using formula, $A= \pi r^2$
3. Accurately weigh 5 gm of sample powder and add to a petri plate.
4. Take a total weight of sample powder with petri plate, record it as W_2
5. Add small quantity of water in petri plate to make slurry of sample.
6. Take weight of slurry with petri plate and record it as W_3.
7. Place petriplate into hot air oven at low temperature 60 °C.
8. Determine and record the weight of sample after 10 min interval till no change in the weight of the sample.
9. Calculate drying rate after each time interval.
10. Plot the curve of drying vs Time and drying vs % moisture content.

Calculations-

Wt of sample with petriplate after drying
Rae of drying= --
Time X Area

Initial Wt of slurry – wt of slurry after drying
Moist content= ---
Initial Wt of slurry – wt of empty clean petri plate

Initial Wt of slurry – wt of slurry after drying
% Moisture content=---X 100
Initial Wt of slurry – wt of empty clean petri plate

Weight loss = Initial Wt of slurry – wt of slurry after drying

Questions for viva-

1. What are the applications of drying?
2. Define bound moisture and unbound moisture.
3. What is triple point?

CHAPTER FIVE

Experiment No.-5

Aim- To construct drying curve for Starch.

Requirements- Spatula, glass rod, pen, pencil, record book, calculator, Graph paper, Hot air oven, petridish, thermometer, weighing balance.

Chemicals- Calcium carbonate

Principle- To behaviour of drying of solid is explained by drying curve. The time required for drying a batch of weight of martial in a dry air can be estimated with the help of drying curve. Drying is a mass transfer process consists of the removal of water or other solvent by evaporations from a solid, semisolid or liquid. This process is obtained used as final production steps before, packing products.

Procedure-

1. Take and weigh empty, clean petri plate and record it as $W_{1.}$
2. Calculate the area of petri plate by using formula, A= πr^2
3. Accurately weigh 5 gm of sample powder and add to a petri plate.
4. Take a total weight of sample powder with petri plate, record it as W_2
5. Add small quantity of water in petri plate to make slurry of sample.
6. Take weight of slurry with petri plate and record it as W_3.
7. Place petriplate into hot air oven at low temperature 60 °C.
8. Determine and record the weight of sample after 10 min interval till no change in the weight of the sample.
9. Calculate drying rate after each time interval.
10. Plot the curve of drying vs Time and drying vs % moisture content.

Questions for Viva-

1. Draw a typical rate of drying curve.
2. Enlist various stages of drying.
3. What is free moisture content and equilibrium moisture content.
4. Classify dryers.
5. Explain drying rate curve.

CHAPTER SIX

Experiment No.-6

Aim- To determine the overall heat transfer coefficient by Heat exchanger.

Requirements- Steam generator, water, condenser (insulated and non-insulated), thermometer, Bent tube

Principle-Consider a heat interchanger, a hot fluid inside a pipe is cooled from T_1 to T_2 by transferring its heat to a cold fluid outside the pipe, entering at t_1 and heated to t_2. Liquid is heated with steam using distillation setup, a temperature gradient exists through the wall between the steam of liquid when steam is condensed it moves through bulb of liquid. The heat is transferred through conduction via film and the surface. The rate of heat transfer is the product of overall heat transfer coefficient area of heating surface & temperature drop.

The overall coefficient may be considered constant throughout the experiment, and specific heat of each fluid may be considered constant, it can be shown

$Q=UA\blacktriangle T_m$

Where, Q= rate of heat transfer

A= area of heating surface

$\blacktriangle T_m$=Mean transfer difference

U=over-all heat transfer coefficient

$\blacktriangle T_m=(\blacktriangle t_2-\blacktriangle t_1)/2.303 \log(\blacktriangle t_2/\blacktriangle t_1)$

$U=Q/A\blacktriangle T_m$

$Q=q_1+q_2,$

q=heat loss by steam,$q1=m1s1 \blacktriangle t_{1+Lm1}$

$q=m_{2}.s_{2}. \blacktriangle t_2$

m_{1}= mass of condensate

s_{1}= specific heat of condensate

L=Latent heat of vaporization of steam (540 cal./A^0)

m_{2}= mass of circulating water

s_{2}=specific heat of circulating water

$\blacktriangle T = (t_2 - t_1)$ temperature drop

t_{2}=temperature of condensate

t_{1}=temperature of outlet

Procedure-

1. Select a steam generator and ensure that it is not having any leak and fill sufficient water.
2. Also select condenser which is having the facility of circulating distillation column.
3. Connect the bend tube of steam generator to the inlet of condenser tube.
4. Connect the outlet of condenser tube to collecting flask in which condensed water is to be collected.
5. Arrange for circulation of cold water around the inner tube of condenser by connecting it to water tap.
6. Also connect the outlet of the inner tube of the condenser to a water collecting drum.
7. Ensure that all the connections and experimental set up is properly made before applying heat to generate steam.
8. Now, heat the water in the steam generator and ensure that steam passes through the condenser tube.
9. Allow the condensation process to continue for about 5 min.
10. Stop the water circulation from the inner tube of the condensate by stopping tap water and put off the heating of water by means of putting off steam generator.
11. Collect circulating water from exit and condensate separately and properly avoiding spillage.
12. Note the temperature of steam and condensate, difference gives the temp drop 't_1'
13. Note the temperature of water at exit and entrance points and difference gives temp. rise 't_2'.
14. Measure volume of condensate collected (M1).
15. Measure volume of water collected (M2).

16. Now calculate average rate of heat transfer (Q) by using equation and determine overall heat transfer coefficient (V) by using equation.
17. Now change speed of circulating water and repeat the whole experiment.
18. Determine overall heat transfer co-efficient.

$$V = \frac{Q}{At}$$

Questions for viva-

1 Define Heat exchangers.

2 Define Heat Interchangers.

3 Name the devices used as Heat Interchangers.

CHAPTER SEVEN

Experiment No. - 7

Aim- Determination of humidity of air by using wet and dry bulb temperatures or psychrometer- use of Dew point method.

Requirements- water, thermometer, beaker, weighing balance, record book, pencil, humidity chart, calculator, burner, psychrometer, cotton, and stand.

Principle: Humidity is defined as pounds of water vapour carried by one pound of dry air under any given set of conditions. The temperature at which air becomes saturated is the wet bulb temperature. At this temperature air is equilibrium with water.

In dew point method, the dew is found on the walls of container at the temperature, where the air is in contact with it, and gets saturated.

In psychrometric method both the dry bulb and wet bulb temperatures are determined. By determining the wet bulb temperature, humidity of dry air and

relative humidity can bre calculated with the help of humidity chart.

Procedure-

A. Dry bulb and wet bulb temperature method-

1. Arrange all the requirements to perform the experiments.
2. Calibrate both the thermometer by using water bath.
3. Fix both the thermometer in psychrometer at wet and dry bulb positions.
4. Place small quantity of water on cotton which is present in water reservoir at bottom of wet thermometer.
5. Rotate the psychrometer inside the laboratory or plate which is under humidity investigation for few temperatures.
6. Record the temperature of dry bulb and wet bulb.
7. Repeat same procedure two more times to have three readings of temperature.
8. Take average of dry and wet bulb temperature.
9. Calculate relative humidity by using humidity chart.

A. **Dew point method-**

1. Collect all the requirements to perform the experiments.
2. Calibrate thermometer by using water bath.
3. Take clean and dried round bottom flask of 100 ml capacity.

4. Fill water in round bottom flask approximately upto 70%of its capacity.
5. Place water filled round bottom flask onto a glass tripod stand.
6. Place calibrated thermometer in water filled round bottom flask but take care that it does not touch to bottom flask.
7. Add small pieces of ice cube into water containing round bottom flask and stirred thoroughly with glass rod.
8. After addition of ice, the temperature of water in RBF is lowered and results into the formulation of mist at the outer bottom surface of the flask.
9. In the psychrometer chart, move the temperature are (X-axis) vertically up until the saturation curve and identify the interesting point of the 'Y' co-ordinate.

Questions for viva-

1. Define psychrometer.
2. Define Dew point.
3. Define Humidity.

CHAPTER EIGHT

Experiment No. 8-

Aim- Description of Construction, working and application of Pharmaceutical Machinery such as rotary tablet machine, fluidized bed coater, fluid energy mill, and dehumidifier.

Requirements- Rotary tablet machine, fluidized bed coater, fluid energy mill, and dehumidifier.

1. Rotary tablet machine- Rotary tablet press is a mechanical device that unlike the single punch tablet press has several tooling station which rotates to compress granules/powder mixture into tablets of uniform size, shape (depending on the punch design) and uniform weight. It was developed to increase the output of tablets. In rotary tablet press, the compaction force on the fill material is exerted by both the upper and lower punches leaving the powder granules to be compressed in the middle. This is known as accordion type of compression. The capacity of a rotary tablet press is determined by the rotation speed of the turrent and the number of stations on the press.

Components/Functional Parts of a Rotary Tablet Press (Multi-Station Tablet Press)-

Hopper- The hopper holds the granules/powder mixture (API plus excipient) that are to be compressed into tablets.

Die cavity – This is where the powder granules are compressed into tablets and it determines. The diameter of the tablet. The size of the tablet to some extent the thickness of the tablet.

Feed paddle – Helps to force the feed/ the granules into the dies especially during faster rotation.

Punches – This comprises the upper and the lower punches. They move within the die bore to compress granules into tablets.

Lower cam track – This guides the lower punch during the filling stage so that the die bore is over filled to allow accurate adjustment.

Cam tracks – This guides the movement of both the upper and lower punches.

Dept of fill/capacity control – This adjusts the lower punch track during the latter part of the fill stage to ensure that the appropriate quantity of granules remains within the die prior to compression.

Recompression rollers – This roller gives the granules an initial compression force to get rid of excess air that might be entrapped in the die.

Main compression – This roller applies the final compression force needed for the formation of tablets.

Ejection cam– Guides the lower punch upwards facilitating the ejection of tablets from the die cavity after compression.

Take-of Blade – This is fitted in front of the feeder housing and it deflects the tablet down the discharge chute.

Discharge chute – This is where the tablet passes through for collection after being deflected by the take-off blade.

Classification of Rotary Tablet Press

Rotary tablet press can be classified into several ways but the most important of these classifications is based on the type of tooling with which the machine is to be used with. A tooling set comprises the die and its associated punches. Basically, there are two types of toolings:

1. "B" type

2. "D" type
The above type of configuration constitutes a majority of the tool configuration used today.

1. **"B" Type**

The "B" type configuration has a normal, punch barrel diameter of 0.750 inches. (19 mm). The "B" type can be used with two types of die or can be said to have two different die sizes:

1. The "B" dies with a diameter of 1.1875 inches. (30.16 mm), suitable for all

   tablet sizes up to the maximum for the "B" punches.

1. The smaller "BB" dies (small "B" die) that has a diameter of 0.945 inches.

   (24 mm). This die type is suitable for tablets up to 9 mm diameter or 11 mm maximum.

"2. D" type

This type has larger nominal barrel diameter of 1 inch. (25.4 mm) and a die diameter of 1.500 inches. (38.10 mm) and thus is suitable for tablets with maximum diameter or maximum length of 25.4 mm.

Tabletting machines are designed to be used with either "B" or "D" tooling but not both. The compression force obtainable in a machine depends on the type of tooling used. Machines that are designed to "B" type tooling exert a maximum compression force of 6.5 tones and machines that use the "D" type configuration exert 10 tones compression force.

There are equally some special machines that are designed with the intention of exerting higher compression forces. The maximum force that can be exerted on a particular size and shape of tablet is governed by the size of the punch tip or the maximum force of which the machine is designed.

Individual manufactures of tablet press have sought to achieve higher output by;

1. Increasing the effective number of punches.

   2. Increasing the number of station.
   3 Increasing the number of points of compression.
   4 . Increasing the rate of compression speed.
   Each of the above approaches has its own advantages and limitations.

Advantages of Rotary Tablet Press (Multi-station tablet press)

1. High productivity can be gained with a minimal amount of labour while

   saving money.

2. Rotary press has an output of between 9000 – 234000 tab/hour thus saves

   time and meets up with the high demand of tablet dosage form.

3. The powder filled cavity can be automatically managed by a moving feeder.

4. Rotary press decreases waste of valuable formulation in non-specific tablets.
5. The machine allows independent control of both weight and hardness.

1. Fluid Bed Coaters are used in coating materials by the fluid bed technology. With fluid bed coating, particles are fluidized and the coating fluid sprayed on and dried. Small droplets and a low viscosity of the spray medium ensure an even product coating.

Advantages-

Uniform, continuous product coating. Aqueous or organic coatings can be applied. Coating and drying take place in one machine.

In terms of Total Containment, the coating process and the filling and emptying of the machine can be carried out in complete isolation and without product spreading into the environment.

When using organic solvents, the process machines can also be made inert and used with a solvent recovery system.

Types

Bottom-Spray Coating-

This processing option uses the energies and controls of the fluid bed to create a pneumatic mass transport inside a special insert, which consists of a perforated bottom screen with defined free areas. Most of the process air is channeled through the center via a tube, as such producing a venturi effect, which sucks the product from outside the partition past the spray nozzle. Leaving the cylindrical partition and entering the conical expansion chamber the particle velocity is dramatically reduced, excess moisture is rapidly evaporated with the dry product returning again and again through the coating zone to receive more coating material. This uniform statistical residence time of all particles in the coating zone results in a very homogenous coating. Due to the high kinetic energy provided by the pneumatic mass flow moist particles are separated, as such allowing the individual coating of even very small particles. Due to the nozzle being positioned directly inside the product and concurrently spraying a premature viscosity change of the coating droplet is avoided. All this features result in the highest possible coating quality, which is imperatively required to produce defined and reproducible drug delivery profiles.

Tangential Spray Coating-

This processing technique is with its physical principles quite similar to bottom-spray coating, only that the production motion is provided by a motor driven rotor disc. Otherwise, the quality producing parameters are the same: Uniform statistical residence time is warranted by defined rotor revolution speed. The coating material is sprayed concurrently inside the rotating product. The rolling motion of the particles provide an even higher separation force, as such preventing agglomeration. However, this high kinetic energy makes it somewhat difficult to coat very small particles and is generally destructive for larger and non-spherical products. The benefits of this processing option are mainly for the layering and subsequent filmcoating of pellets.

Top-Spray Coating-

This processing option is frequently used by the food, feed and chemical industries as the function of the film mainly serves to improve the general handling or storage times, i.e. time limited protection against moisture, oxygen or light. A perfect film is generally not required for this function, but care must be taken that the droplets do not become too viscous before touching the substrate, in order to maintain a good spreadability. As however neither the particle motion, nor the travel distance of droplet from nozzle to substrate are uniform the film structure is generally rather porous, but nevertheless measuring up to the above described requirements.

1. Fluidized Energy mill

Fluidized Energy mill, also known as micronizer or jet mill is a type of mill that consists of a hollow toroid that has a diameter of 20-200 mm depending on the height of the loop which can be up to 2 m. It operates by particle impaction and attrition.

A fluid or milling gas, usually air or inert gas is injected as a high-pressure jet through nozzles at the bottom of the loop. The powder particles in the mill are accelerated to high velocity.

The kinetic energy of the air plus the turbulence created causes interparticle (particle-particle collision) and particle-wall contact resulting in particle size between 2 and 10 micrometers. The fluidized effect transports the particles to a classification zone where the size classifier retains the particles until sufficiently fine to be removed.

Pharmaceutical uses of Fluidized Energy mill

a. Fluidized energy is used in milling thermolabile materials

b. It is the choice of mill when a higher degree of drug purity is required

c. Fluidized energy mill is used for the fine grinding of frits, Kaolin, Zircon, titanium, and calcium, alumina.

Advantages of Fluidized Energy mill

1. The machine has no moving parts and thus the tendency of contamination due to wear of parts is minimized.
2. The equipment is easily sterilized.
3. Small particle size (between 2 and 10) is usually obtained at the end of milling.

4. Thermolabile materials can be milled with little degradation since the heat produced by the process is nullified by the cooling effect of the expansion of the compressed gas.

Disadvantages of Fluidized Energy mill

1. Tendency of forming aggregates or agglomerates after milling.
2. Generation of amorphous content due to high energy impact.
3. Formation of ultra-fine particles

4. Dehumidifier-

A **dehumidifier** is an air conditioning device which reduces and maintains the level of humidity in the air. This is done usually for health or thermal comfort reasons, or to eliminate musty odor and to prevent the growth of mildew by extracting water from the air. It can be used for household, commercial, or industrial applications. Large dehumidifiers are used in commercial buildings such as indoor ice rinks and swimming pools, as well as manufacturing plants or storage warehouses. Typical air conditioning systems combine dehumidification with cooling, by operating cooling coils below the dewpoint and draining away the water that condenses.

Construction-

Components of humidifier-

1. Cold evaporator coil
2. Warm condenser coil
3. A fan
4. Reservior to catch water

Working- A humidifier uses principle same as way of air conditions but doesn't cool air, infact it warm air. Warm air from structure is drawn into the cold humidification coil for humidifier. Then temperature of air is lower below point. During humidifier process, heat is produced as water vapour become liquid. This total heat then collected by refrigenrant system along with the heat taken is collected as heat energyand added to refrigerant. Latent heat and compression heat then transfer by refrigerant system to the condenser coil.

Applications-

1. It lower the relative humidity to handling of hygroscopic material.
2. It lower the new point to lower condensation.
3. Provide protective atmosphere for heat treatment.
4. Control humidity in warehouse.
5. Preserve ships,

Questions for Viva-

1. List componenets of Rotary tablet Press.
2. Advantages of Rotary tablet press machine.
3. Define Humidifier.
4. Give Components of Humidifier.

CHAPTER NINE

Experiment No. 9

Aim- To evaluate size distribution of tablet granulations,Construction of various size frequency curves including arithmetic and logarithmic probability plots

Requirements- set of standard sieve, bottom pan, and sieve shaker, weighing balance, butter paper, paper sheet, pencil and notebook.

Principle- Sieve method gives sieve diameter, sieve diameter is defined as the diameter of the sphere that possess through the sieve aperture as the asymmetric particle sieve method directly give weight distribution. Particles having size range from 50 and 1500µm are estimated by sieving method. In this method, the size is expressed as dsieve. The sieving method finds application in dosage and development of tablets and capsules. Normally 15 percent of fine powder (passed through mesh 100) should be present in granulated material to get a proper flow of material and achieve good compaction in tableting. Therefore, percent of coarse and fine can be quickly estimated. Sieves for pharmaceutical testing are constructed from wire cloth with square meshes, woven from wire of brass, bronze, stainless steel or any other suitable

material.

Procedure-

1. Clean the sieve and empty collecting pan.
2. Set the sieves in ascending order and with collecting pan positioned at bottom.
3. Weigh the granules or sample under study and put it on the uppermost sieve.
4. Keep the complete set of sieves filled with the sample material on the sieve shaker and close with lid.
5. Set the sieve shaker at right speed and sieving time.
6. Now start the sieve shaker.
7. When the sieving time has expired each sieve, collect the particles retained on each sieve.
8. Calculate average particle size as per formula.

$$\%\ \text{weight retained} = \frac{\text{Weight of powder retained on sieve}}{\text{Total weight of powder taken for experiment}}$$

CHAPTER TEN

Experiment- No. 10

Aim- To verify the laws of size reduction using ball mill and determining Kicks, Rittinger's, Bond's coefficients, power requirement and critical speed of Ball Mill

Requirements- Calcium carbonate powder, Ball mill with balls, butter paper, paper sheet, pencil, notebook.

Procedure-

1. The metal balls to be used in mill should be washed and cleaned.
2. Take 100 g calcium carbonate and loaded into ball mill.
3. Weigh the given sample and obtain the initial size distribution by sieving.
4. Grind the sample in the ball mill for 30 min.
5. Sieve the powder through sieve no 10, measure the size distribution by sieving.
6. The remaining sample is again transferred into the container.
7. Again operate the ball mill for 60 min.
8. The powder is again sieve through sieve no. 16.
9. Determine average particle size.

Questions for viva-

1. Define size reduction.
2. What is fine powder?
3. What is coarse powder?
4. Give principle of Ball mill.

CHAPTER ELEVEN

Experiment No. 11

Aim- Demonstration of colloid mill, planetary mixer, fluidized bed dryer, freeze dryer.

1. **Colloid mill-**

Principle- colloid mill consists of two steel discs having very small clearance between them. One disc is rotating, while the other one is stationary. When the material is passed through these discs, they get sheared. Thus coarse particles are broken down into small particles due to shear.

Construction-

A colloidal mill consists of high speed rotor and stator with a conical miling surface. The miling surface may be smooth surface. Rough surface mills are used for fibrous material because fibres tend to inter lock and clog smooth surfaced mills. The clearance between rotor and stator can be adjusted from 0.05 to o.75 mm . during milling the heat generated may rise the temperature upto 40°c. Hence cold water circulation is provided to reduce the temperature as much as 20°c. The discharge pipe is also connected to hopper, so that discharge can be recycled.

Working-

Materials for the manufacture of suspensions and emulsions are placed in a hopper, usually the solids are premilled to prevent the damage of colloid mill. The solids are mixed with the liquid vehicle before introducing into the colloid mill. The dispersion flows down and adheres to the rotor. During the movement of rotor (3000 to 20000 rpm). centrifugal force throws a part the dispersion on the stator. Thus size reduction can be achieved. The milled liquid may be recycled. After achieving the desired size, discharge is collected from outlet in the periphery of the housing.

Normally, the size of milled particles may be smaller than the clearance, because of the force of high shear. In emulsification, clearance of 75 micron may produce dispersion with an average particles size of 3 micron.

The capacities of colloid mills range from 2 to 3 L/min for smaller mills and 440 L/ min for the larger mills.

Application-

1. The main use of colloid mill is dispersion of solid particles within liquid.
2. It is used to reduce particles size in suspension in liquid or to reduce droplet size of liquid suspended in another liquid.
3. It is frequently used to increase the stability of suspensions and emulsions.
4. It is mainly used in pharmaceutical purpose for preparations, colloidal dispersions, suspensions, emulsions and ointments.
5. Particles size of as small as 3 microns can be obtained by the colloidal mill.
6. Fibrous materials can be milled using rough surface rotor and stator.

1. **Planetary Mixer-**

Principle- In a planetary mixer the blade tears the mass apart and shear is applied between moving blade and stationary wall. The mixing arm moves in two ways, around its own axis and around the central axis, so that it reaches every spot of the vessel. The plates in the blade are sloped so that the powder makes an upward movement. Therefore, tumbling motion is also obtained.

Construction- It consists of a vertical cylindrical shell, which can be removed either by lowering it beneath the blade or raising the blade above the bowl. The mixing blade is mounted from the top of bowl. The making shaft is driven by a planetary gear train. It rotates around the ring gear which further rotates round the mixer blade. It is normally built with variable speed drive.

Working- In the planetary mixer, the agitator has planetory motion. It rotates on its own axis and around the central axis so that it reaches all parts of the vessel. Beaker is shaped to pass with close clearance over the side and bottom of the mixing bowl. The blade tears the mass apart and shear is applied between the moving blade and stationary wall. The plates in the blade are sloped so that the powder makes an upward movement. Therefore tumbling (convective) motion is also obtained. Since it is a variable speed driven. Initially the blade moves slowly for premixing and finally at increased speed for active mixing. Thus, high shear can be applied for mixing.

Emptying the bowl may be done by hand or by dumping mechanism.

Applications-

1. It is used for the preparation of creams, gels and light viscous fluid.
2. It produces precise blends in addition to breaking down of agglomerates rapidly.
3. Low speeds are used for dry blending and faster speeds for the kneading action required in wet granulation.
4. Steam jacketed bowls are used in manufacture of sustained released product and ointments.

3. **Fluidized bed dryer-**

Principle- Fluidized bed dryer are used in the pharmaceutical industries to reduce moisture content of pharmaceutical powders and granules. They also use in the drying of suspension, slurries, solutions, dilute paste or sludge.

Construction- The dryer is made of stainless steel or plastic. A detachable bowl is placed at the bottom of the dryer, which is used for chraging and discharging. The bowl has a perforated bottom with a wire mesh support for placing materials to be dried. A fan is mounted in the upper part for circulating hot air. Fresh air inlet, prefiller and heat exchanger are connected serially to heat the air to the required temperatures. The temperature of hot air and exist are monitored. Bag filters are placed above the drying bowl for recovery of fines.

Working-

1. Clean the bag by using double distilled water and dry it. Clean other parts of fluidized bed dryer.
2. Take suitable quantity of prepared granules as per capacity of FBD and low into trolley.
3. Fix the trolly at apparatus position and at the bottom of equipment.
4. Switch on the instrument and allow the fresh and hot air to enter into bag.
5. Wait for some time still whole particles are not dried.

6. Unload the content from trolley and determine moisture content by balance method.

Application-

1. Fluidized bed dryer is popularly used for drying of granules in the production of tablets.
2. It is used for mixing , granulation and drying.

4 Freeze Dryer- Freeze drying is process water is frozen, followed by its removel from sample, initially by sublimation (primary drying) and then by desorption (secondary drying).

Principle- The main principle involved in freeze drying is a phenomenon called sublimation. Where water passes directly from solid state (ice) to the vapor state without passing through the liquid state. The material to be dried is first frozen and then subjected under high vaccum to heat. So that frozen liquid sublimes leaving only solid, dried components of original liquid.

Construction- A freezę dryer or lyphilizer consists of-

1. A vaccum chamber or product chamber or manifold
2. Sample are placed on the shelves within the vaccum chamber.
3. Process condenser designed to trap the solvent which is usually water, during the drying process. The process condenser will consist of coils or sometimes plates which are refrigerated to allow temperature.
4. Shelf fluid system, the freeze drying process requires that product is first frozen and then energy in form of heat is applied through out drying phase of cycle.
5. Refrigeration system, the product to be freeze dried is either frozen before into dryer or frozen whilst on the shelves.
6. Vaccum system, to remove solvent reasonable time, vaccum must be during the drying process.
7. Control system, comtrol may be entirely or usually fully automatic for production machines.

Working- The freeze drying process consists of following steps.

1. Preparation and pretreatment- The volume of solution is introduced into the container is limited by its capacity. Satisfactory freeze drying beyond certain limit of depth of liquid is not possible. Therefore pretreatment is essential. The solution is pre-concentrated under normal vaccum tray drying. Final product becomes more porous.
2. Prefreezing to solidify water- vials, ampoules or bottles in which the aqeous solution is packed are frozen in cold shelves (about 50°C). During this stage, cabinet is maintained at low temperature and atmospheric pressure. The normal cooling rate is about 1 to 3 kelvin per minute so that large ice crystals with relatively large holes are formed on sublimation of ice.
3. Primary drying (sublimation of ice under vaccum)-

As the drying proceeds, thickness of the frozen layer decreases and the thickness of partially dried solid increases. Primary drying stage removes easily removable moisture. During this stage about 98% to 99% water is removed

4. Secondary drying (Removal of residual moisture under high vaccum)- During this stage, traces of moisture is removed. The temperature of solid is raised to as high as 50 to 60°C, but vaccum is lowered that is used in primary drying. The rate of drying is very low and it takes about 10 to 20 hours.
5. Packing- After vaccum is replaced by inert gas, the bottles and vials are closed.

Applications-

1. Freeze drying process is used as to increase the shelf life of products, such as vaccines and other injectables.
2. Freeze drying is used to preserve food and make it very light weight.
3. In chemical synthesis, products are often freeze-dried to make them more stable or easier to dissolve in water for subsequent use.
4. In bio-separations, freeze drying can be used for late stage purification procedure , because it can effectively remove solvents.

Questions for Viva-

1. Give applications of colloid mill.
2. Give use of planetary mixer.
3. Give types of fluidized bed dryer.
4. What is lyophilization?

CHAPTER TWELVE

Experiment No. 12

Aim- To study the effect of concentration on rate of filtration.

Requirements-

Powder sample, calcium carbonate, beaker , funnel, stop clock, butter paper, filter paper sheet.

Principle:

Filtration is a process of where by solid particles present in a suspension are separated from the liquid or gas employing a porous medium. Which retains the solid but allows the fluid to pass through the volume of the filtrate obtained through the filter paper per unit time is called "**rate of filtration**" can be given by mathematical equation.

dv/dt = K.A . $\triangle$P/µL – darcy's law

where,

A = area of filter

$\triangle$**P** = pressure drop across the filter medium and cake

µ = viscosity of filtrate

L = thickness of cake

V = volume of the filtrate

T = time taken for filtration

K = constant for the filter medium and filter cake or resistance

Procedure-

1. Weigh calcium carbonate powder accurately and transfer to graduated conical flask, make concentration of water(50ml) and calcium carbonate as 0gm, 0.5gm 1gm, 1.5gm, 2gm, 2.5gm and 3gm concentrations.
2. Shake each flask and label it serially from 1to 7.
3. Assembled the filtration assembly of funnel and filter paper, pass the solutions through filtration assembly one by one and record the time taken for complete filtration in seconds and minutes.
4. Repeat same procedure for all remaining flasks solution and record the time taken for filtration (use new sheet of filter paper during filtration of each sample).
5. Calculate the rate of filtration by using formula given below

Volume of filtration in ml

Rate of filtration= ---

Time taken in (min)

Questions for Viva-

1. Define filtration.
2. Enlist types of filtration.
3. Define filter medium.
4. What is rate of filtration?
5. State Darcy's law?

CHAPTER THIRTEEN

Experiment No.-13

Aim- To study the effect of viscosity (Thickness) on rate of filtration.

Requirement-

Measuring cylinder, beaker, glass rod, stop watch, filter paper, weighing balance, butter paper, funnel

Chemicals- Acetone, Glycerine, castor oil water.

Principle:

Filtration is a process of where by solid particles present in a suspension are separated from the liquid or gas employing a porous medium. Which retains the solid but allows the fluid to pass through the volume of the filtrate obtained through the filter paper per unit time is called "**rate of filtration**" can be given by mathematical equation.

$dv/dt = K.A \,.\, \triangle P/\mu L$ – darcy's law

where,

A = area of filter

$\triangle$P = pressure drop across the filter medium and cake

μ = viscosity of filtrate

L = thickness of cake

V = volume of the filtrate

T = time taken for filtration

K = constant for the filter medium and filter cake or resistance

Procedure-

1. Assemble the filtration assembly of funnel and filter paper.
2. Pass the 50 ml of water through it and record the time to complete filtration in second or minute.
3. Repeate the above mentioned procedure for all remaining samples (such as acetone, glycerine, castor oil).
4. Record the time for filtration and note it down.
5. Calculate the rate of filtration.
6. Plot the graph of viscosity of sample on x-axis vs rate of filtration on y-axis.

Questions for Viva-

1. Define filter aid.
2. What is filter cake?
3. What is filtrate?
4. State poiseuilles's law of filtration.
5. What is filter leaf?
6. Define clarification.

CHAPTER FOURTEEN

Experiment No.-14

Aim- To study the effect of surface area on rate of evaporation.

Requirements-

Thermometer, water bath, weighing balance, tripod stand, glass rod.

Chemicals- Sodium chloride, calcium chloride, glycerine.

Principle- Evaporation is simply vaporization from the surface of a liquid. Vaporization of a liquid below its boiling point is called evaporation. When heat is applied to the solution, it is absorbed and the motion of molecules increases. The energy absorbed by water molecules during evaporation, is used to give them the motion needed to escape the surface of the liquid that is the molecule present in the surface overcome the surface tension of the liquid. That is the molecules present in surface overcome and evaporate. This heat is referred to as the heat of vaporization. As a result of evaporation the remaining water is reduced and water becomes cool.

Procedure-

1. Assemble the water bath on tripod stand and set the assembly in such way that burner flame should reach to the water bath.
2. Measure internal diameter of three beakers of same size and calculate surface area.
3. Add 50ml of water in each beaker and take weight of each beaker separately.
4. Place all beakers in water bath and keep the temperature of water bath upto 80^0C.
5. Record the weight of beaker with water after each 20 min interval upto period of 1 hour.

Questions for viva-

1. Define Evaporation.
2. Give objectives of evaporation.
3. Give applications of evaporation.
4. Enlist the factors influencing evaporation.

CHAPTER FIFTEEN

Experiment No-15

Aim- To study the effect of time on rate of crystallization.

Requirement-

Measuring cylinder, beaker, weighing balance, water bath, funnel, filter paper

Chemicals- Potassium nitrate, Ice bath

Principle- When the concentration of a compound in its solution is greater than the solubility of that compound in that solvent that condition is known as supersaturation. This is an unstable state, from that supersaturated solution the excess compound is supersaturated or crystallize. When the temperature of supersaturated solution is decreased rapidly, the solubility of solute decreases, As a result, the dissolved solid gets crystallize through the process of necleation and crystal growth. The extent of crystallization depends on the time on contact in low temperature.

Procedure-

Weigh 75 g of potassium nitrate accurately.

1. Transfer 100 ml of water into 250ml of beaker.
2. Place the beaker in constant temperature maintained water bath at 50^0C.
3. Add potassium nitrate into water in small small quantities, simultaneously stir the solution with glass rod to dissolve solute.
4. Continue the process until saturated solution is formed.
5. Then transfer 10ml of saturated solution into 9 beakers.
6. Place all the beakers in an ice bath, When temperature of the solution decreases suddenly

Question for Viva-

1. Define crystallization.
2. Enlist steps involved in crystallization.
3. Define supersaturation.
4. Define Nucleartion.
5. Give objectives of Crystallization.

CHAPTER SIXTEEN

Experiment No.-16

Aim- To calculate the uniformity index for given sample by using Double cone blender

Requirements-

Double cone blender, weighing balance, spectrophotometer

Chemicals-

Paracetamol, talk powder, sodium hydroxide, glycerine, acetone.

Principle- Mixing may be defined as a unit operation that tends to results in a randomization of dissimilar particles within a system. Whenever a product contains more than one components a mixing stage will be required. To discuss the principles of the mixing process, a situation will be considered where there are equal quantities of two powdered components of the same size, shape and density that required to be mixed.

Procedure-

1. Clean the double cone blender with double distilled water and swab it with cotton soaked in acetone.
2. Prepare calibration curve of drug paracetamol in 0.1 N NaOH at 257 nm by using double beam spectrophotometer and calculate y=mx+C1
3. Weigh accurately 10 gm of paracetamol and 90 gm of talk powder.
4. Add above mentioned ingredients in the blender and close the lid.
5. Switch on the blender and rotate at the speed of 20 rpm for the period 30 min.
6. After 30 min. of mixing stop the machine and withdraw 1 gm of the sample from top middle and bottom portion of the blender.
7. All the samples are subjected to elimination of content paracetamol in % by using spectrophotometer as per pharmacopeial method.
8. Note all the readings of 1% of paracetamol and calculate the uniformity index.

Questions for viva-

1. Define mixing,
2. Enlist the factors affecting mixing.
3. Give uses of double cone blender.
4. Give advantages of double cone blender.

9 798889 599715

Printed by Libri Plureos GmbH in Hamburg,
Germany